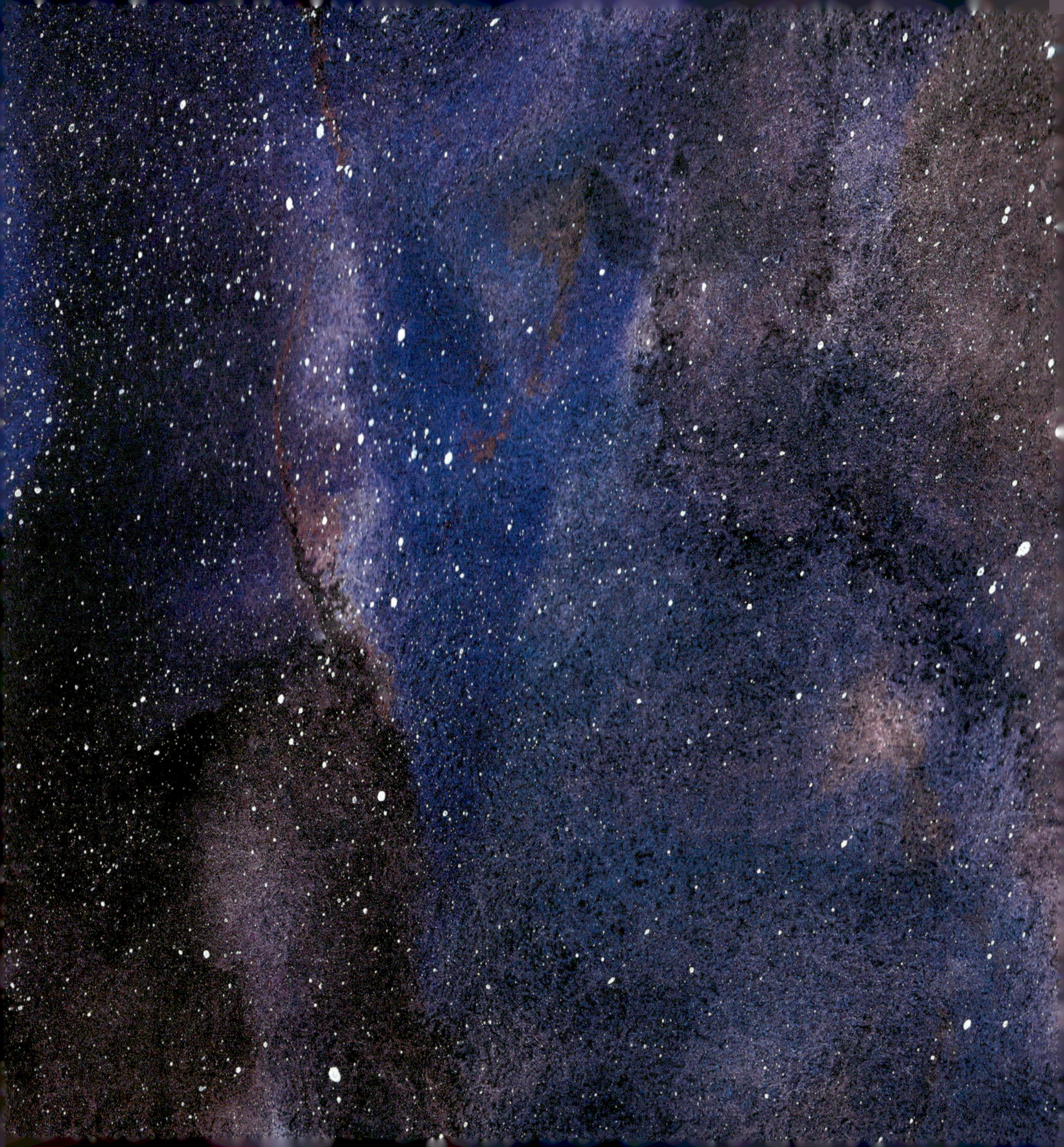

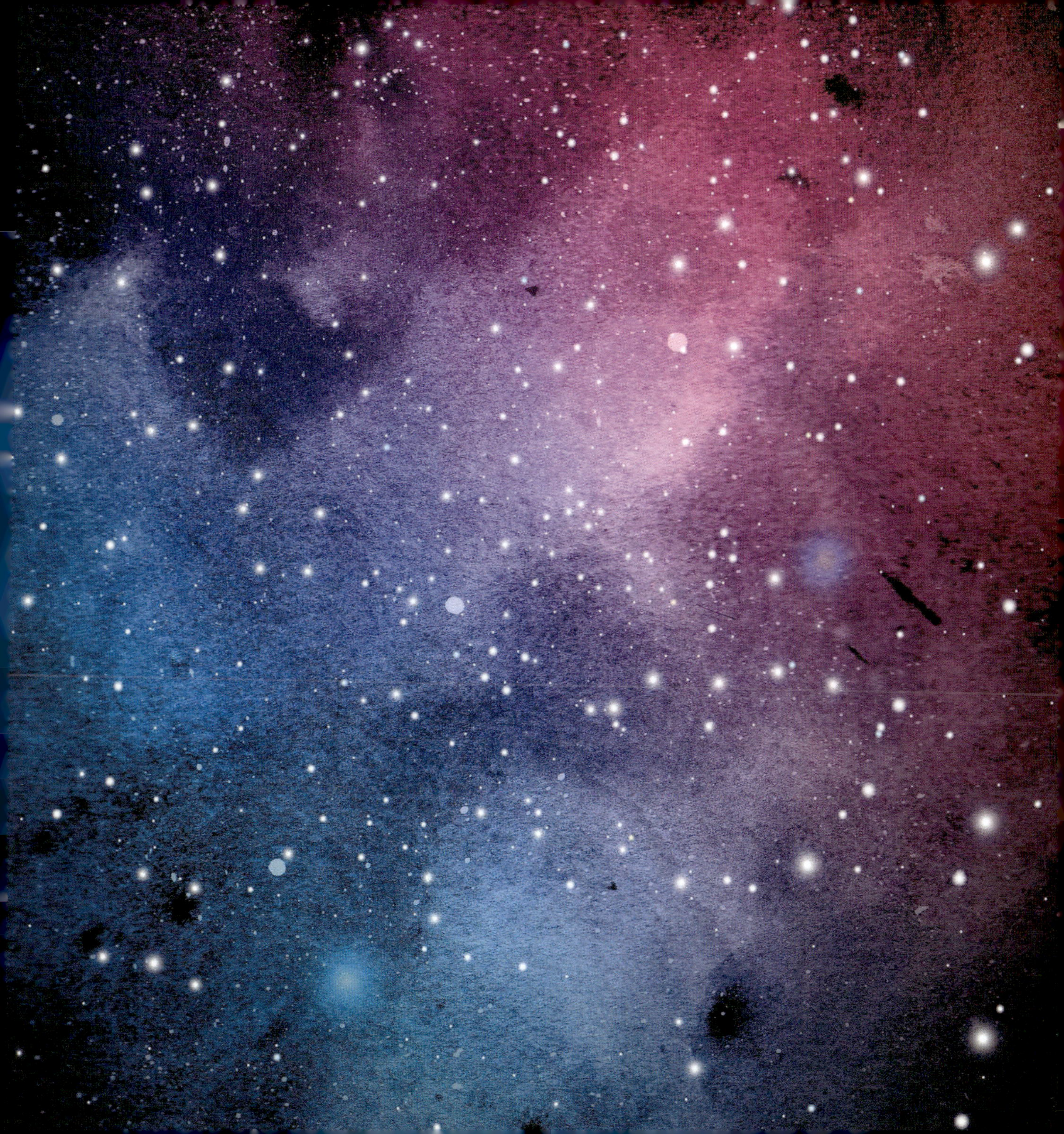

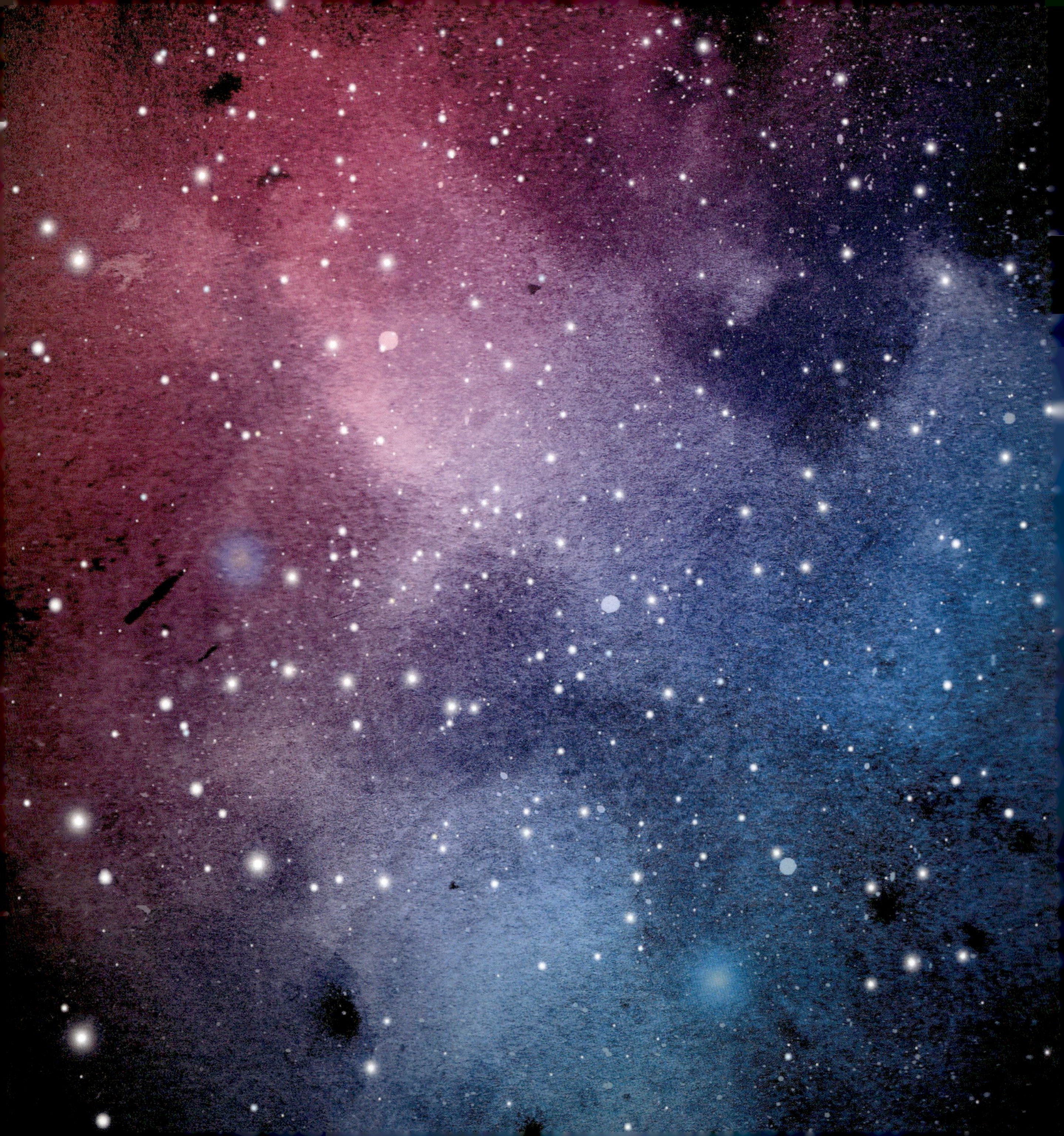

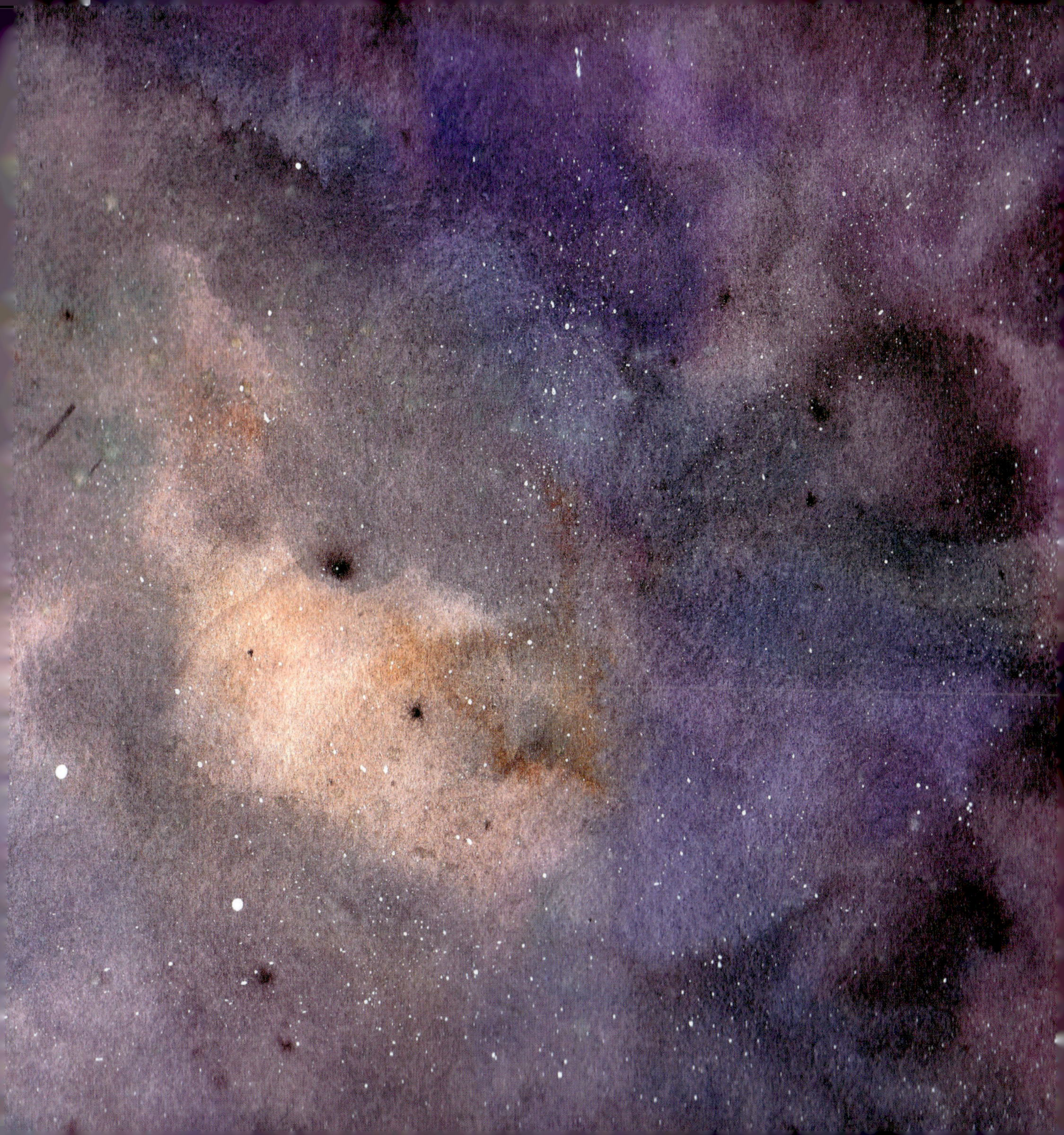

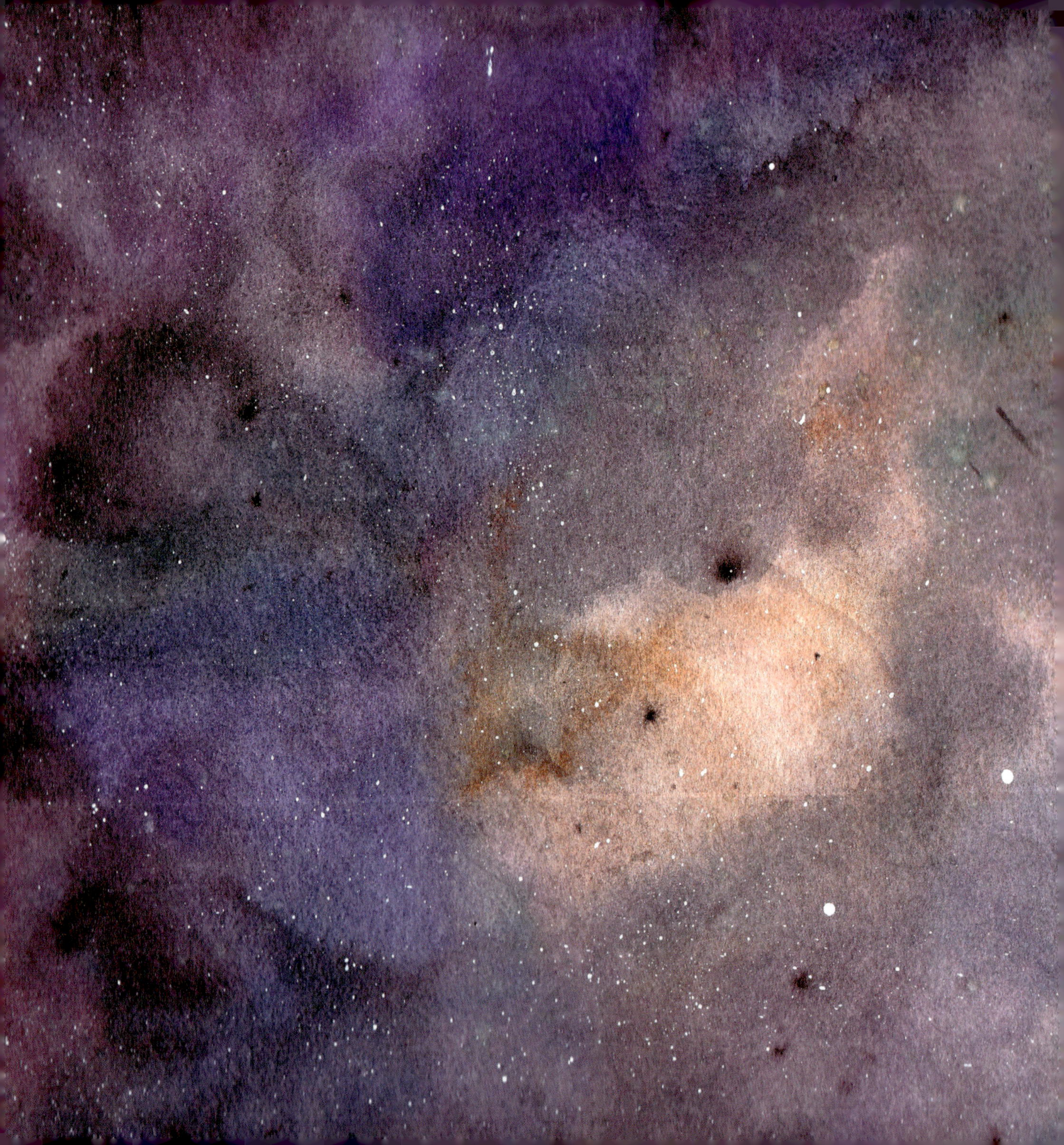

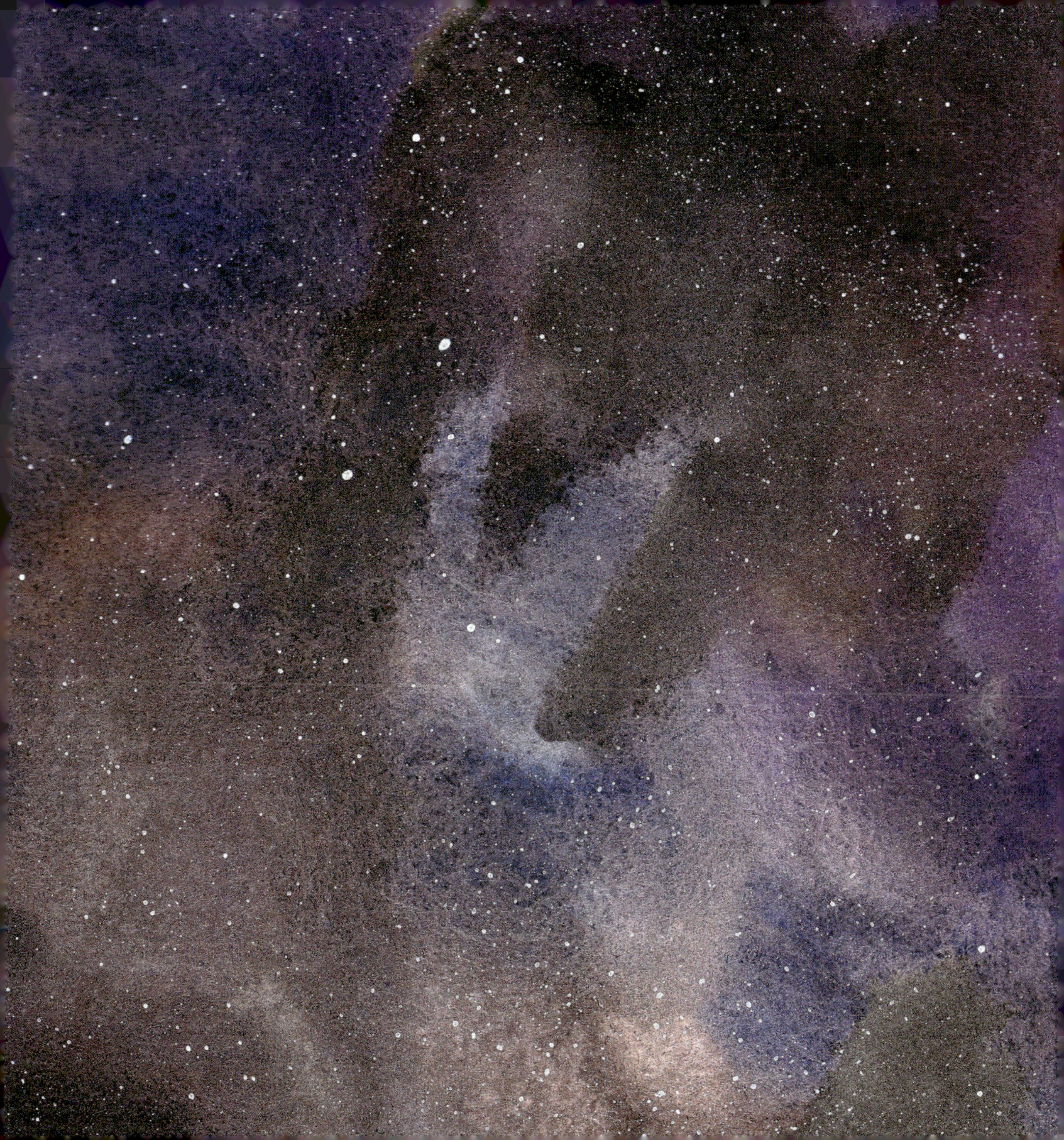

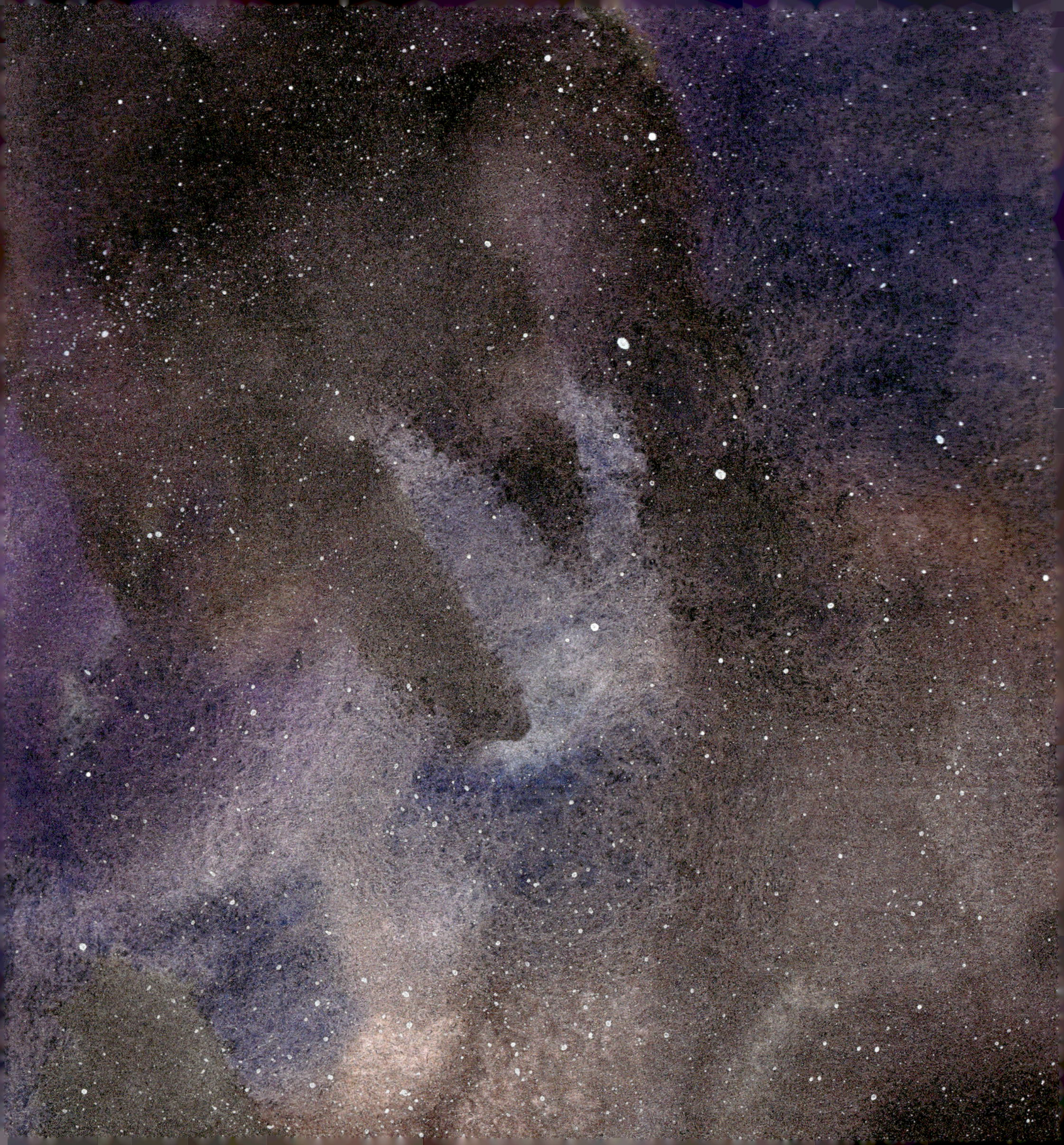

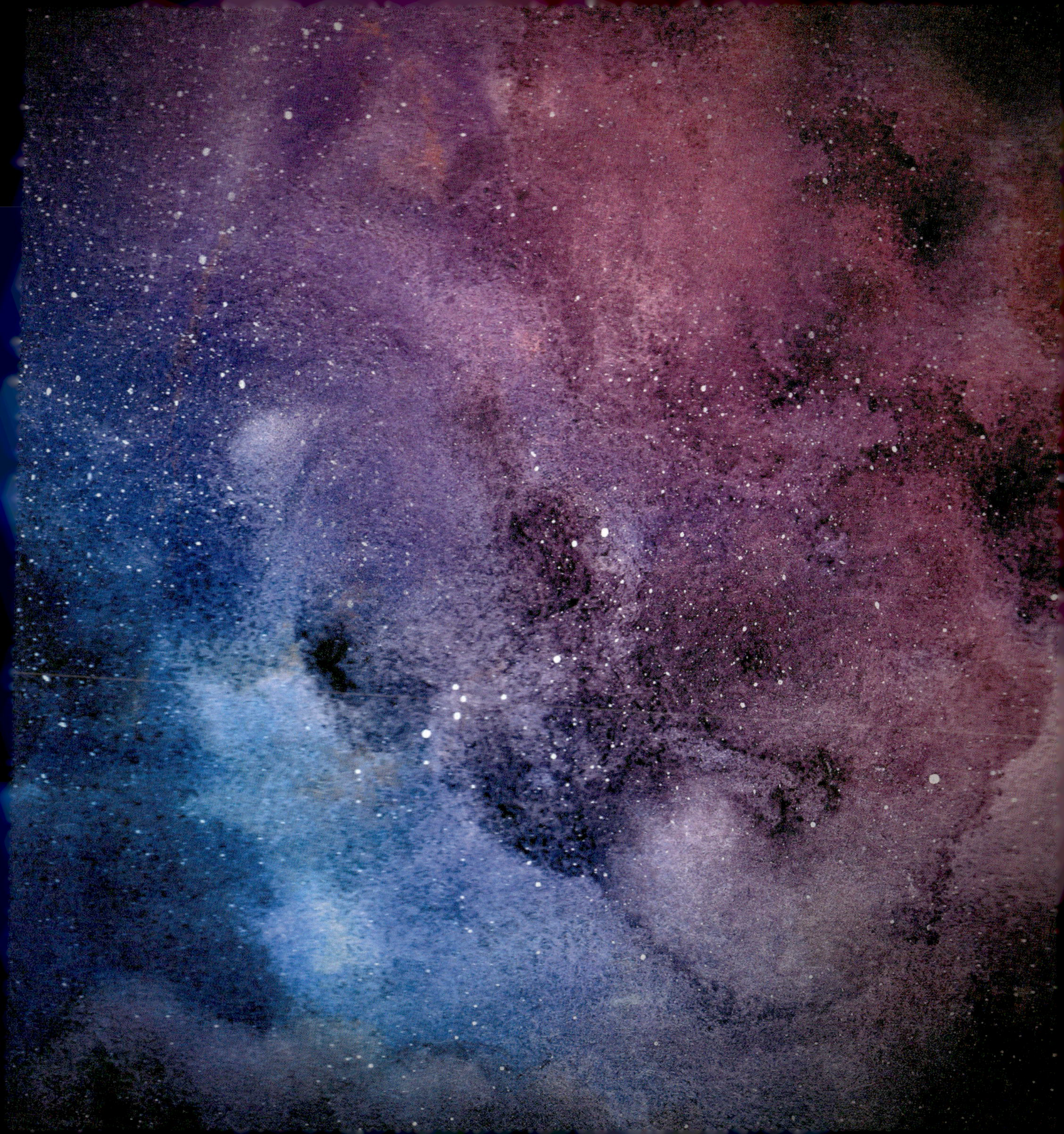

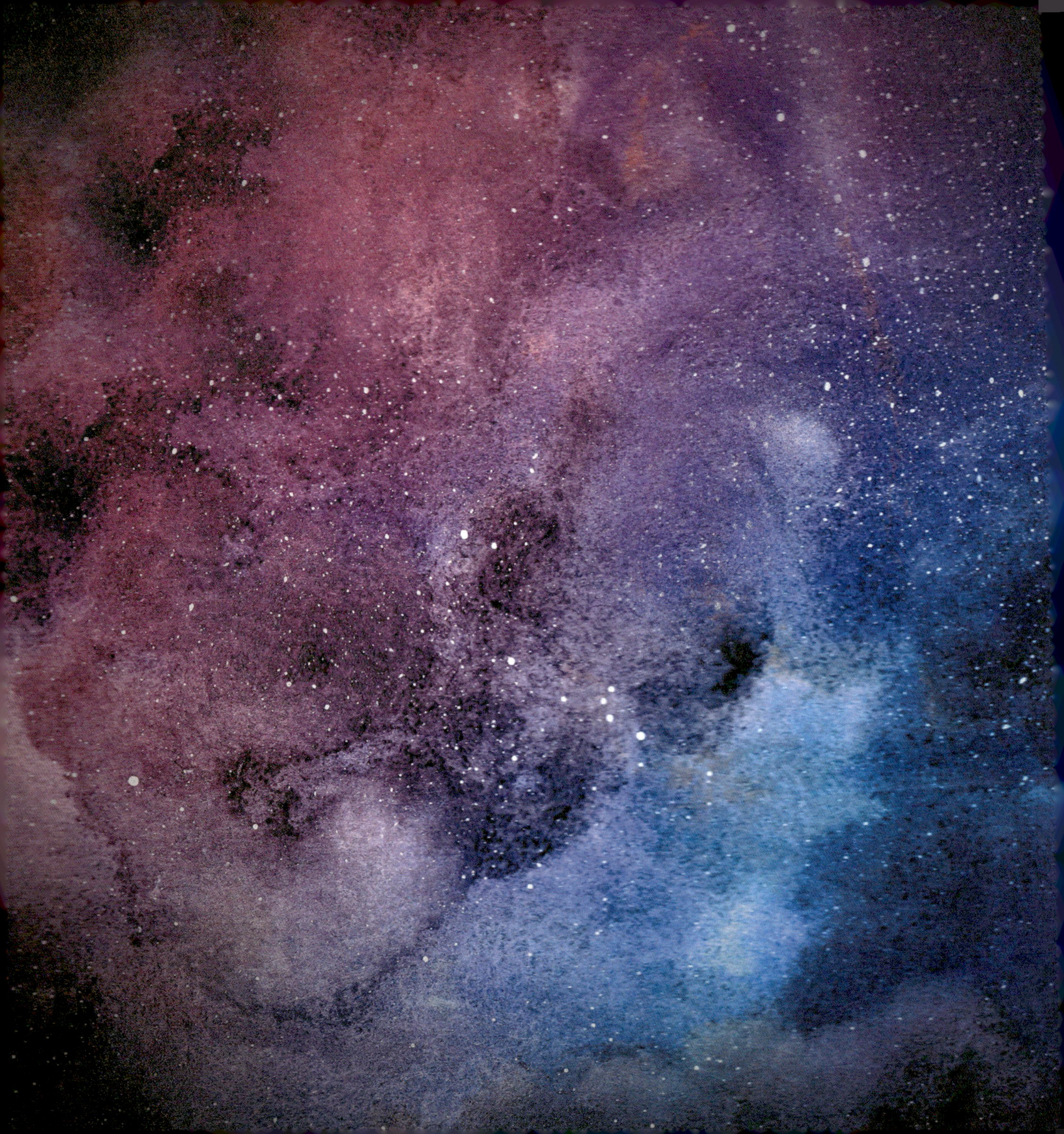

Printed in Great Britain
by Amazon

74326929R00015